Get Your **FREE** Digital Version by Scanning the Code Below!

SCAN ME

TABLE OF CONTENTS

HOW TO PLAY

TO PLAY THIS AWESOME GAME, YOU NEED AT LEAST 2 PLAYERS AND SOME PENCILS FOR LATER.

THE YOUNGEST PLAYER MUST START WITH THE FIRST QUESTION. IF HE/SHE IS TOO YOUNG TO READ THEN THE SECOND YOUNGEST WILL SUFFICE!

EACH PLAYER TAKES TURNS READING THESE SUPER ICKY QUESTIONS ALOUD WHILE TRYING THEIR BEST NOT TO BE SICK!

REMEMBER TO EXPLAIN WHY YOU CHOOSE YOUR ANSWER IN THE SILLIEST WAY IMAGINABLE. WHOEVER GIVES THE BEST ANSWER GETS A POINT.

IF YOU MAKE THE OTHER PLAYER LAUGH WITH YOUR ANSWER THEN YOU GET LAUGHTER POINTS, YOU GET TWO LAUGHTER POINTS PER QUESTION!

SO IF YOU WIN A NORMAL POINT AND TWO LAUGHTER POINTS THEN YOU GET THREE POINTS FOR ONE QUESTION!

IF YOUR ANSWER IS NOT THE BEST BUT YOU WERE FUNNY, YOU CAN STILL GET POINTS!

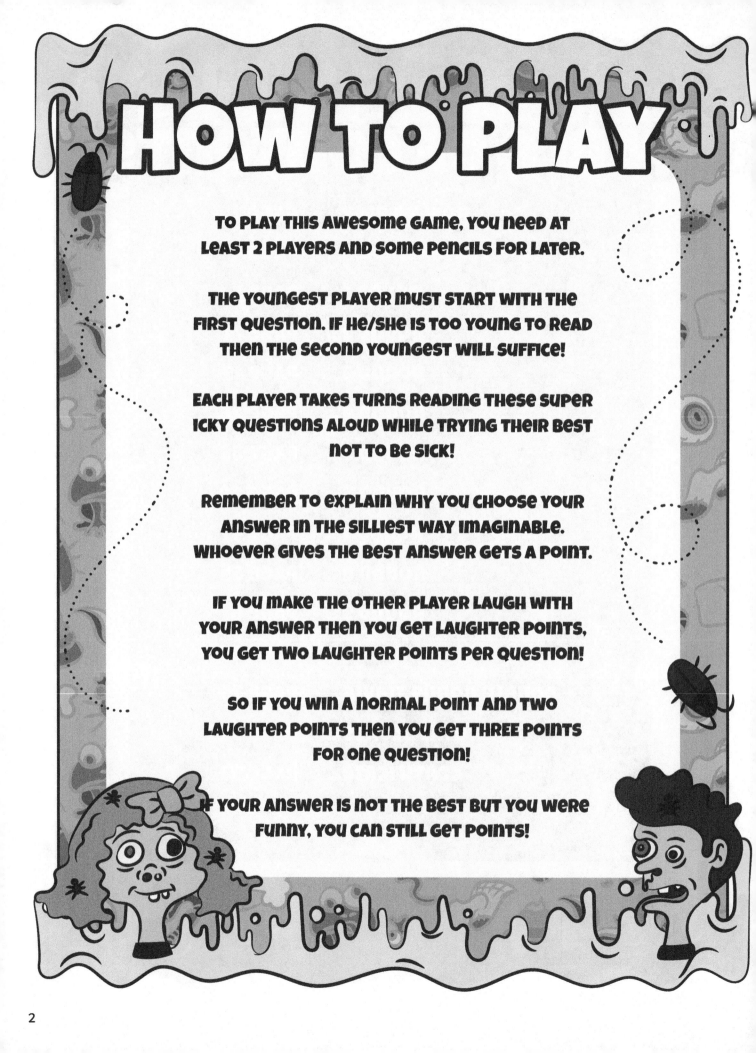

HOW TO PLAY

THE TRIVIA QUESTIONS COUNT FOR DOUBLE POINTS FOR THE EXPLANATION & LAUGHTER POINTS, SO THERE IS A CHANCE FOR SIX POINTS PER QUESTION! DON'T BE AFRAID TO ACT THE CLASS CLOWN IF YOU WANT THOSE POINTS!

THERE ARE TEN ROUNDS OF TWENTY QUESTIONS, WITH EACH ROUND GRADUALLY BECOMING MORE AND MORE ICKY AND GROSS! MAKE SURE YOU HAVE A SICK BUCKET READY!

AT THE END OF THE GAME, WHOEVER HAS THE MOST POINTS IS THE LEGENDARY LEADER OF LAUGHTER AND SHOULD BE WORSHIPED AS THE LAUGHTER GOD THAT THEY ARE!

THERE IS A PAGE AT THE END OF EACH ROUND WHERE PLAYERS CAN COUNT UP THEIR POINTS AND SEE WHO IS THE ULTIMATE COMEDIAN!

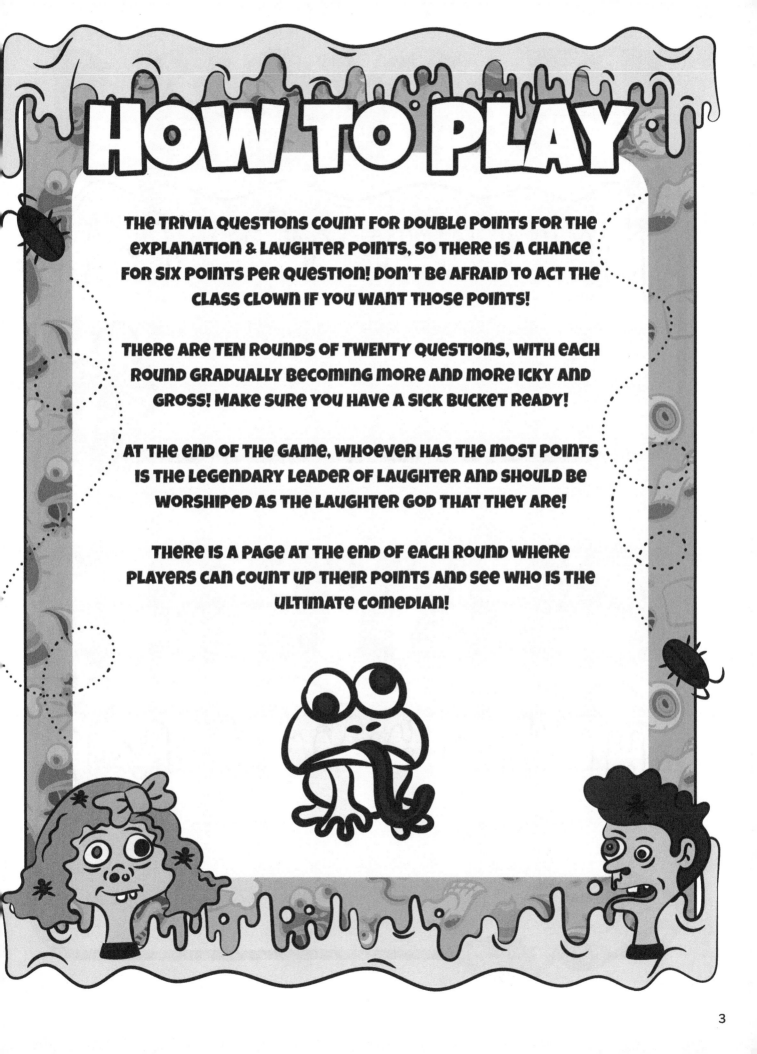

PLAYER 1

PLAYER 2

ROUND 1: EASY PEASY Lemon SQUEEZY

1. WOULD YOU RATHER... HAVE A SHOWER IN TOMATO KETCHUP OR IN VERY STICKY HONEY?

Player 1   Question Points _____ Laugh Points _____
Player 2   Question Points _____ Laugh Points _____

2. WOULD YOU RATHER...SLEEP ON THE BUTT OF AN ELEPHANT OR THE BUTT OF A DONKEY?

Player 1   Question Points _____ Laugh Points _____
Player 2   Question Points _____ Laugh Points _____

3. WOULD YOU RATHER...KISS 10 FROGS IN 1 MINUTE OR LICK 5 RATS IN 30 SECONDS?

Player 1   Question Points _____ Laugh Points _____
Player 2   Question Points _____ Laugh Points _____

4. WOULD YOU RATHER...FALL INTO A PIT FULL OF SMELLY SOCKS OR BRUSH YOUR TEETH WITH AN ONION RING?

Player 1   Question Points _____ Laugh Points _____
Player 2   Question Points _____ Laugh Points _____

5. WOULD YOU RATHER...KISS SOMEONE AFTER THEY ATE GARLIC OR AFTER THEY DRANK PRUNE JUICE?

Player 1   Question Points _____ Laugh Points _____
Player 2   Question Points _____ Laugh Points _____

6. WOULD YOU RATHER...GET WOKEN UP BY A LOUD FART OR FALL ASLEEP TO THE SOUND OF BURPS?

Player 1   Question Points _____ Laugh Points _____
Player 2   Question Points _____ Laugh Points _____

7. WOULD YOU RATHER...EAT A BOWL OF FINGERNAILS OR A BOWL OF TOENAILS?

Player 1   Question Points _____ Laugh Points _____
Player 2   Question Points _____ Laugh Points _____

8. WOULD YOU RATHER... HAVE TO LICK EVERY PERSON YOU MEET OR GREET THEM WITH A BIG LOUD FART?

Player 1   Question Points _____ Laugh Points _____
Player 2   Question Points _____ Laugh Points _____

9. WOULD YOU RATHER...SNOT CAME OUT OF YOUR NOSE WHEN YOU ATE, OR YOU BURPED EVERY TIME YOU TALKED?

Player 1   Question Points _____ Laugh Points _____
Player 2   Question Points _____ Laugh Points _____

10. WOULD YOU RATHER...IT RAINED USED DIAPERS OR DOG POOP ONCE A WEEK?

Player 1   Question Points _____ Laugh Points _____
Player 2   Question Points _____ Laugh Points _____

11. WOULD YOU RATHER...CHECK A DOG FOR FLEAS OR PICK TICKS OFF OF A GORILLA?

Player 1   Question Points _____ Laugh Points _____
Player 2   Question Points _____ Laugh Points _____

12. WOULD YOU RATHER...USE YOUR TOOTHBRUSH AFTER A DOG LICKED IT OR USE YOUR HAIRBRUSH AFTER IT WAS IN KITTY LITTER?

Player 1   Question Points _____ Laugh Points _____
Player 2   Question Points _____ Laugh Points _____

13. WOULD YOU RATHER...DRINK CABBAGE JUICE OR ONION JUICE FIRST THING IN THE MORNING?

Player 1   Question Points _____ Laugh Points _____
Player 2   Question Points _____ Laugh Points _____

14. WOULD YOU RATHER...EAT IN A ROOM FULL OF FARTS OR FULL OF SMELLY CATS AND DOGS?

Player 1   Question Points _____ Laugh Points _____
Player 2   Question Points _____ Laugh Points _____

15. WOULD YOU RATHER...USE A DIRTY RUG OR A STUFFED BEAVER AS A TOWEL AFTER A SHOWER?

Player 1   Question Points _____ Laugh Points _____
Player 2   Question Points _____ Laugh Points _____

16. WOULD YOU RATHER...HAVE YOUR NEXT BIRTHDAY PARTY CLOSE TO AN OPEN SEWER OR INSIDE A RUBBISH DUMP?

Player 1   Question Points _____ Laugh Points _____
Player 2   Question Points _____ Laugh Points _____

17. WOULD YOU RATHER...HAVE ANTS CONSTANTLY IN YOUR PANTS OR WORMS ALWAYS IN YOUR SHOES?

Player 1   Question Points _____ Laugh Points _____
Player 2   Question Points _____ Laugh Points _____

18. WOULD YOU RATHER...HAVE ALL YOUR SOCKS FILLED WITH SLUGS OR FILLED WITH MAGGOTS?

Player 1   Question Points _____ Laugh Points _____
Player 2   Question Points _____ Laugh Points _____

19. WOULD YOU RATHER...HAVE TOILET PAPER MADE OF STINGING NETTLES OR POISON IVY?

Player 1   Question Points _____ Laugh Points _____
Player 2   Question Points _____ Laugh Points _____

20. WOULD YOU RATHER...HAVE A BLOCKED TOILET FOR A WEEK OR NO RUNNING WATER FOR A MONTH?

Player 1   Question Points _____ Laugh Points _____
Player 2   Question Points _____ Laugh Points _____

PLAYER 1

Round Total

PLAYER 2

Round Total

ROUND CHAMPION

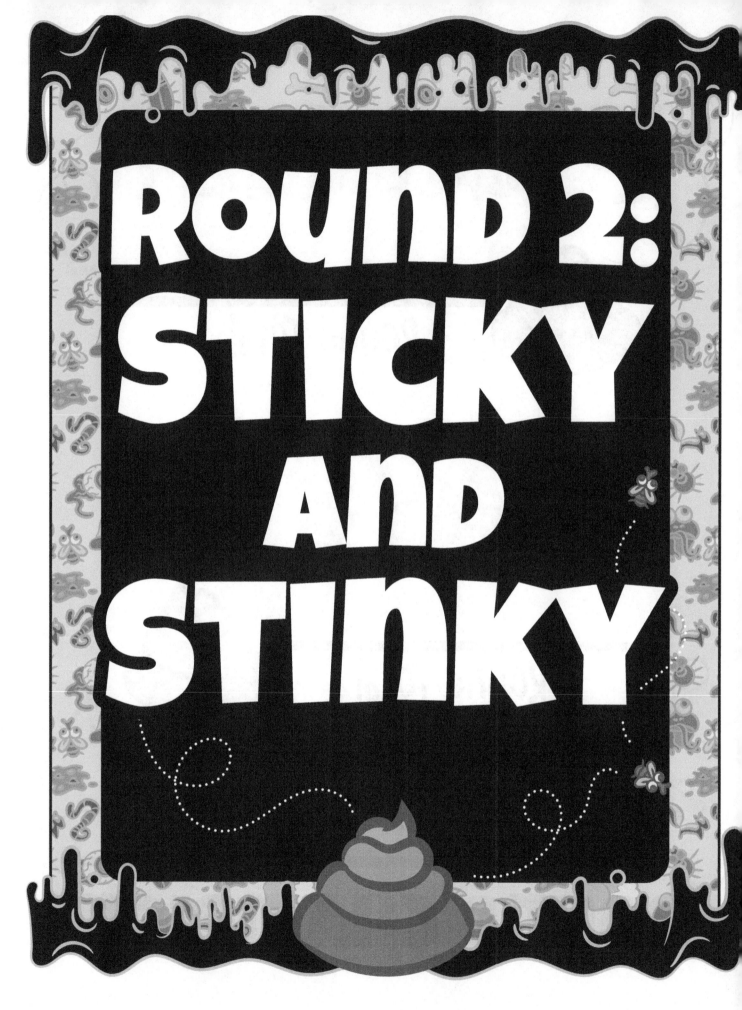

ROUND 2: STICKY AND STINKY

1. WOULD YOU RATHER...WEAR PERFUME MADE FROM COW POOP OR FROM DOG VOMIT?

Player 1   Question Points _____ Laugh Points _____
Player 2   Question Points _____ Laugh Points _____

2. WOULD YOU RATHER...HAVE A BLOWHOLE THAT SQUIRTED JELLY EVERY 2 MINUTES OR A LONG TONGUE YOU COULDN'T FIT IN YOUR MOUTH?

Player 1   Question Points _____ Laugh Points _____
Player 2   Question Points _____ Laugh Points _____

3. WOULD YOU RATHER...LET STRAY DOGS SLEEP IN YOUR BED OR RATS RUNNING AROUND YOUR HOUSE?

Player 1   Question Points _____ Laugh Points _____
Player 2   Question Points _____ Laugh Points _____

4. WOULD YOU RATHER...MAKE FRIED SLUGS FOR BREAKFAST OR EAT ONE GIANT UNCOOKED SNAIL FOR LUNCH?

Player 1   Question Points _____ Laugh Points _____
Player 2   Question Points _____ Laugh Points _____

PLAYER 1 _____   PLAYER 2 _____

5. WOULD YOU RATHER...SUCK ON GARLIC CLOVES FOR 5 MINUTES OR EAT A WHOLE ONION IN 1 MINUTE?

Player 1   Question Points _____ Laugh Points _____
Player 2   Question Points _____ Laugh Points _____

6. WOULD YOU RATHER...SHOWER IN SYRUP OR IN BACON FAT?

Player 1   Question Points _____ Laugh Points _____
Player 2   Question Points _____ Laugh Points _____

7. WOULD YOU RATHER...ALL TAP WATER WAS DARK BROWN OR GLOWED NEON GREEN?

Player 1   Question Points _____ Laugh Points _____
Player 2   Question Points _____ Laugh Points _____

8. WOULD YOU RATHER...YOU ALWAYS SMELLED BAD, OR YOUR BEDROOM ALWAYS SMELLED BAD?

Player 1   Question Points _____ Laugh Points _____
Player 2   Question Points _____ Laugh Points _____

9. WOULD YOU RATHER...ABSORB BAD SMELLS ANYWHERE YOU WENT OR COULD NEVER SMELL ANYTHING BAD?

Player 1   Question Points _____ Laugh Points _____
Player 2   Question Points _____ Laugh Points _____

10. WOULD YOU RATHER... COMMUNICATE ONLY BY FARTING OR BY BURPING?

Player 1   Question Points _____ Laugh Points _____
Player 2   Question Points _____ Laugh Points _____

11. WOULD YOU RATHER...EVERYWHERE YOU WALKED WAS STICKY OR EVERYTHING YOU TOUCHED WAS GLOOPY?

Player 1   Question Points _____ Laugh Points _____
Player 2   Question Points _____ Laugh Points _____

12. WOULD YOU RATHER...WALK AROUND SMELLING LIKE A WET DOG OR SMELLING LIKE OUT-OF-DATE MILK?

Player 1   Question Points _____ Laugh Points _____
Player 2   Question Points _____ Laugh Points _____

13. WOULD YOU RATHER...SWEATED ONCE EVERY 30 MINUTES OR SNEEZED EVERY 20 MINUTES?

Player 1   Question Points _____   Laugh Points _____
Player 2   Question Points _____   Laugh Points _____

14. WOULD YOU RATHER...YOUR ARMPITS ALWAYS SMELLED OR YOUR FEET ALWAYS SMELLED?

Player 1   Question Points _____   Laugh Points _____
Player 2   Question Points _____   Laugh Points _____

15. WOULD YOU RATHER...YOU HAD TO BUY NEW CLOTHES EVERY DAY BECAUSE YOU WERE SO SMELLY OR GIVE PEOPLE FACE MASKS TO HANDLE YOUR NEVER-ENDING SMELL?

Player 1   Question Points _____   Laugh Points _____
Player 2   Question Points _____   Laugh Points _____

16. WOULD YOU RATHER... BE AS STICKY AS GLUE OR AS STINKY AS POO?

Player 1   Question Points _____   Laugh Points _____
Player 2   Question Points _____   Laugh Points _____

17. WOULD YOU RATHER...SNEEZE POOP OR FART SNOT?

Player 1   Question Points _____ Laugh Points _____
Player 2   Question Points _____ Laugh Points _____

18. WOULD YOU RATHER...YOUR SWEAT OR YOUR FARTS WERE SUPER TOXIC?

Player 1   Question Points _____ Laugh Points _____
Player 2   Question Points _____ Laugh Points _____

19. WOULD YOU RATHER...YOUR HOUSE WAS MADE OF USED DIAPERS OR OF GONE OFF YOGURT?

Player 1   Question Points _____ Laugh Points _____
Player 2   Question Points _____ Laugh Points _____

20. WOULD YOU RATHER...BATHE WITH ONIONS AND GARLIC OR IN A BLUE CHEESE SAUCE?

Player 1   Question Points _____ Laugh Points _____
Player 2   Question Points _____ Laugh Points _____

PLAYER 1

_____
Round Total

PLAYER 2

_____
Round Total

_____
ROUND CHAMPION

ROUND 3: GROSS THINGS YOU FORGOT EXISTED

1. WOULD YOU RATHER...never use YOUR PHONE WHILE ON THE TOILET OR never POP A SPOT ON YOUR FACE?

Player 1   Question Points _____ Laugh Points _____
Player 2   Question Points _____ Laugh Points _____

2. WOULD YOU RATHER...NOT SHOWER FOR A WEEK OR BRUSH YOUR TEETH FOR 3 DAYS?

Player 1   Question Points _____ Laugh Points _____
Player 2   Question Points _____ Laugh Points _____

3. WOULD YOU RATHER...SCRATCH YOUR BUTT INTENSELY OR PICK YOUR NOSE IN PUBLIC?

Player 1   Question Points _____ Laugh Points _____
Player 2   Question Points _____ Laugh Points _____

4. WOULD YOU RATHER...WIPE EYE GUNK OR CLEAN YOUR EARS AT THE DINNER TABLE?

Player 1   Question Points _____ Laugh Points _____
Player 2   Question Points _____ Laugh Points _____

5. WOULD YOU RATHER...HAVE LOTS OF GROSS GUNK UNDER YOUR FINGERNAILS OR A BELLY BUTTON FULL OF FLUFF?

Player 1   Question Points _____ Laugh Points _____
Player 2   Question Points _____ Laugh Points _____

6. WOULD YOU RATHER...SMELL OTHER PEOPLE'S FINGERS OR SMELL YOUR OWN FEET DURING BREAKFAST?

Player 1   Question Points _____ Laugh Points _____
Player 2   Question Points _____ Laugh Points _____

7. WOULD YOU RATHER...WIPE YOUR STINKY ARMPITS WITH A DIRTY CLOTH OR WEAR SUPER-STRONG DEODORANT?

Player 1   Question Points _____ Laugh Points _____
Player 2   Question Points _____ Laugh Points _____

8. WOULD YOU RATHER...EAT A WEEK-OLD COOKIE OR DRINK A GLASS OF SOUR CREAM?

Player 1   Question Points _____ Laugh Points _____
Player 2   Question Points _____ Laugh Points _____

9. WOULD YOU RATHER...SNEEZE ALL OVER A PARENT OR SPIT A HUGE LOOGIE IN FRONT OF AN AUDIENCE?

Player 1   Question Points _____ Laugh Points _____
Player 2   Question Points _____ Laugh Points _____

10. WOULD YOU RATHER...REMOVE THE DEAD SKIN FROM A PARENT'S FEET OR LET A DOG LICK YOU CLEAN?

Player 1   Question Points _____ Laugh Points _____
Player 2   Question Points _____ Laugh Points _____

11. WOULD YOU RATHER...DIG FOR FOOD IN YOUR TEETH WITHOUT WASHING YOUR HANDS OR EAT SOMETHING THAT WAS ON THE GROUND?

Player 1   Question Points _____ Laugh Points _____
Player 2   Question Points _____ Laugh Points _____

12. WOULD YOU RATHER...REUSE EARBUDS OR REUSE DENTAL FLOSS?

Player 1   Question Points _____ Laugh Points _____
Player 2   Question Points _____ Laugh Points _____

13. WOULD YOU RATHER...SHARE A DEODORANT STICK WITH YOUR WHOLE FAMILY OR HAVE EVERYONE'S CLOTHES WASHED TOGETHER?

Player 1   Question Points _____ Laugh Points _____
Player 2   Question Points _____ Laugh Points _____

14. WOULD YOU RATHER...DRINK FROM A DIRTY GLASS OR EAT WITH DIRTY CUTLERY?

Player 1   Question Points _____ Laugh Points _____
Player 2   Question Points _____ Laugh Points _____

15. WOULD YOU RATHER...USE THE SAME TOWEL FOR A MONTH OR NEVER WEAR SOCKS FOR A WEEK?

Player 1   Question Points _____ Laugh Points _____
Player 2   Question Points _____ Laugh Points _____

16. WOULD YOU RATHER...SLEEP IN THE CLOTHES YOU HAD BEEN WEARING ALL DAY OR GO TO WORK WITHOUT HAVING A SHOWER?

Player 1   Question Points _____ Laugh Points _____
Player 2   Question Points _____ Laugh Points _____

17. WOULD YOU RATHER...never do laundry for 2 weeks or never use shampoo for a month?

Player 1   Question Points _____ Laugh Points _____
Player 2   Question Points _____ Laugh Points _____

18. WOULD YOU RATHER...use tree leaves or banana peels as toilet paper?

Player 1   Question Points _____ Laugh Points _____
Player 2   Question Points _____ Laugh Points _____

19. WOULD YOU RATHER...use the same toothbrush for a year or share one bar of soap with your family?

Player 1   Question Points _____ Laugh Points _____
Player 2   Question Points _____ Laugh Points _____

20. WOULD YOU RATHER...sleep in a bed full of crumbs or sit on a couch covered in dog hair?

Player 1   Question Points _____ Laugh Points _____
Player 2   Question Points _____ Laugh Points _____

PLAYER 1

_____
Round Total

PLAYER 2

_____
Round Total

_____
ROUND CHAMPION

ROUND 4: ALL ABOUT SMELLS

1. WOULD YOU RATHER... HAVE AIR CON THAT FARTED OR AN OVEN THAT BURPED?

Player 1   Question Points _____ Laugh Points _____
Player 2   Question Points _____ Laugh Points _____

2. WOULD YOU RATHER...YOUR GARDEN WAS USED AS A LANDFILL, OR STRAY CATS USED YOUR HOUSE AS ONE BIG LITTER BOX?

Player 1   Question Points _____ Laugh Points _____
Player 2   Question Points _____ Laugh Points _____

3. WOULD YOU RATHER...YOUR GROUND FLOOR WAS COMPLETELY COVERED IN STINKY MUD OR IN DOG HAIR?

Player 1   Question Points _____ Laugh Points _____
Player 2   Question Points _____ Laugh Points _____

4. WOULD YOU RATHER... DRINK A SMOOTHIE MADE FROM ROTTEN FRUIT OR EAT A 5-DAY OLD KEBAB?

Player 1   Question Points _____ Laugh Points _____
Player 2   Question Points _____ Laugh Points _____

5. WOULD YOU RATHER...WASH YOUR FACE WITH VINEGAR OR SHOWER IN PRUNE JUICE?

Player 1   Question Points _____ Laugh Points _____
Player 2   Question Points _____ Laugh Points _____

6. WOULD YOU RATHER... EAT NOTHING BUT CHEESE FOR A WEEK OR NEVER EAT CHEESE FOR A YEAR?

Player 1   Question Points _____ Laugh Points _____
Player 2   Question Points _____ Laugh Points _____

7. WOULD YOU RATHER...USE GARLIC FLAVORED TOOTHPASTE OR CABBAGE FLAVORED MOUTHWASH?

Player 1   Question Points _____ Laugh Points _____
Player 2   Question Points _____ Laugh Points _____

8. WOULD YOU RATHER... LET A SKUNK SPRAY YOU OR SPRAY YOUR FAMILY?

Player 1   Question Points _____ Laugh Points _____
Player 2   Question Points _____ Laugh Points _____

9. WOULD YOU RATHER... VOMIT EACH TIME YOU SMELLED CHOCOLATE OR FART EACH TIME YOU ATE CHOCOLATE?

Player 1   Question Points _____ Laugh Points _____
Player 2   Question Points _____ Laugh Points _____

10. WOULD YOU RATHER...WASH YOUR CAR IN CAT URINE OR TAKE A BATH IN BAKED BEANS?

Player 1   Question Points _____ Laugh Points _____
Player 2   Question Points _____ Laugh Points _____

11. WOULD YOU RATHER... FIND 1 MILLION DOLLARS UNDER A PILE OF USED DIAPERS OR INSIDE A DEAD WHALE?

Player 1   Question Points _____ Laugh Points _____
Player 2   Question Points _____ Laugh Points _____

12. WOULD YOU RATHER... HAVE BAD BREATH, OR EVERYONE YOU KNOW HAD BAD BREATH?

Player 1   Question Points _____ Laugh Points _____
Player 2   Question Points _____ Laugh Points _____

13. WOULD YOU RATHER...ALL YOUR CLOTHES SMELLED OF CIGARETTE SMOKE OR SMELLED OF SPICY FARTS?

Player 1   Question Points _____ Laugh Points _____
Player 2   Question Points _____ Laugh Points _____

14. WOULD YOU RATHER...WASH OUT A DIRTY GARBAGE CAN OR BUY A NEW ONE?

Player 1   Question Points _____ Laugh Points _____
Player 2   Question Points _____ Laugh Points _____

15. WOULD YOU RATHER...WAKE UP WITH DOG BREATH OR SUPER STINKY FEET?

Player 1   Question Points _____ Laugh Points _____
Player 2   Question Points _____ Laugh Points _____

16. WOULD YOU RATHER... EAT A CURRY OR DRINK GRAVY EVERY DAY FOR A WEEK?

Player 1   Question Points _____ Laugh Points _____
Player 2   Question Points _____ Laugh Points _____

17. WOULD YOU RATHER...HAVE A NAP INSIDE A HUGE TUNA SANDWICH OR SWIM IN A POOL OF ONION SOUP?

Player 1   Question Points _____ Laugh Points _____
Player 2   Question Points _____ Laugh Points _____

18. WOULD YOU RATHER...ALL FURNITURE IN YOUR HOUSE WAS FOUND IN A DUMPSTER OR HAVE NO FURNITURE AT ALL?

Player 1   Question Points _____ Laugh Points _____
Player 2   Question Points _____ Laugh Points _____

19. WOULD YOU RATHER...SCOFF 20 HARD-BOILED EGGS OR DRANK 3 BOWLS OF CABBAGE SOUP IN ONE SITTING?

Player 1   Question Points _____ Laugh Points _____
Player 2   Question Points _____ Laugh Points _____

20. WOULD YOU RATHER...HAVE A MUSHROOM PIZZA SCENTED CANDLE OR A CHEESEBURGER SCENTED CANDLE?

Player 1   Question Points _____ Laugh Points _____
Player 2   Question Points _____ Laugh Points _____

PLAYER 1

Round Total

PLAYER 2

Round Total

ROUND CHAMPION

ROUND 5: EWWWW!

1. WOULD YOU RATHER... EAT AT A DINNER TABLE COVERED IN 2-DAY OLD KETCHUP OR EAT FROM A VERY CLEAN TOILET SEAT?

Player 1   Question Points _____   Laugh Points _____
Player 2   Question Points _____   Laugh Points _____

2. WOULD YOU RATHER...LICK ALL DIRTY PLATES AND CUTLERY CLEAN OR NEVER USE ANY CUTLERY AND PLATES TO EAT?

Player 1   Question Points _____   Laugh Points _____
Player 2   Question Points _____   Laugh Points _____

3. WOULD YOU RATHER...PUT CHEWED GUM IN YOUR POCKET OR HAVE PRAWNS IN YOUR HAIR?

Player 1   Question Points _____   Laugh Points _____
Player 2   Question Points _____   Laugh Points _____

4. WOULD YOU RATHER... FIND A HAIR IN YOUR FOOD OR EAT WITHOUT USING YOUR HANDS?

Player 1   Question Points _____   Laugh Points _____
Player 2   Question Points _____   Laugh Points _____

5. WOULD YOU RATHER... YOU GOT HIT BY BIRD POOP OR STOOD ON DOG POOP EVERY TIME YOU LEFT YOUR HOME?

Player 1   Question Points _____ Laugh Points _____
Player 2   Question Points _____ Laugh Points _____

6. WOULD YOU RATHER...LISTEN TO THE SOUND OF LOUD CHEWING OR LOUD COUGHING FOR AN HOUR?

Player 1   Question Points _____ Laugh Points _____
Player 2   Question Points _____ Laugh Points _____

7. WOULD YOU RATHER...WIPE YOUR FACE WITH GREASY CHICKEN SKIN OR RUB BUTTER ON YOUR LEGS?

Player 1   Question Points _____ Laugh Points _____
Player 2   Question Points _____ Laugh Points _____

8. WOULD YOU RATHER...WATCH YOUR WHOLE FAMILY LICK THEIR FINGERS AFTER DINNER OR EAT DINNER WITH THEIR HANDS TIED BEHIND THEIR BACK?

Player 1   Question Points _____ Laugh Points _____
Player 2   Question Points _____ Laugh Points _____

9. WOULD YOU RATHER...PUT WATER IN YOUR CEREAL OR MAYONNAISE ON YOUR TOAST FOR BREAKFAST?

Player 1   Question Points _____ Laugh Points _____
Player 2   Question Points _____ Laugh Points _____

10. WOULD YOU RATHER...CLEAN YOUR PHONE SCREEN BY SPITTING ON IT OR WASH YOUR CLOTHES USING ONLY SOAP?

Player 1   Question Points _____ Laugh Points _____
Player 2   Question Points _____ Laugh Points _____

11. WOULD YOU RATHER...EAT A STEAK THAT HAS BEEN SNEEZED ON OR EAT A WHOLE RAW POTATO?

Player 1   Question Points _____ Laugh Points _____
Player 2   Question Points _____ Laugh Points _____

12. WOULD YOU RATHER...STICK YOUR HAND INSIDE A CROCODILE'S MOUTH OR PUT YOUR FEET INTO A FOOT SPA OF PIRANHAS?

Player 1   Question Points _____ Laugh Points _____
Player 2   Question Points _____ Laugh Points _____

13. WOULD YOU RATHER...YOUR WHOLE FAMILY ATE FROM A PIG TROUGH OR EVERYONE FART AND BURPED DURING EVERY MEALTIME?

Player 1   Question Points _____ Laugh Points _____
Player 2   Question Points _____ Laugh Points _____

14. WOULD YOU RATHER...USE CHEESE SAUCE AS SUN LOTION OR WASP REPELLENT AS HAIR SPRAY?

Player 1   Question Points _____ Laugh Points _____
Player 2   Question Points _____ Laugh Points _____

15. WOULD YOU RATHER...HAVE A FACIAL SNAIL TREATMENT OR A SNAKE MASSAGE?

Player 1   Question Points _____ Laugh Points _____
Player 2   Question Points _____ Laugh Points _____

16. WOULD YOU RATHER... VISIT A TAXIDERMY MUSEUM ON A HOT DAY OR GO ON A TOUR IN A SEWAGE PLANT?

Player 1   Question Points _____ Laugh Points _____
Player 2   Question Points _____ Laugh Points _____

17. WOULD YOU RATHER... CHILL IN A HORSE MANURE FILLED JACUZZI OR RELAX IN A STEAM ROOM POWERED BY FARTS?

Player 1   Question Points _____   Laugh Points _____
Player 2   Question Points _____   Laugh Points _____

18. WOULD YOU RATHER...HAVE TO EAT YOUR LEAST FAVORITE FOOD OR HAVE A SEVERE ALLERGY TO YOUR FAVORITE THING TO EAT?

Player 1   Question Points _____   Laugh Points _____
Player 2   Question Points _____   Laugh Points _____

19. WOULD YOU RATHER...YOU COULD SEE EVERY TYPE OF GERM OR SMELL BAD ODORS THAT ARE FAR AWAY?

Player 1   Question Points _____   Laugh Points _____
Player 2   Question Points _____   Laugh Points _____

20. WOULD YOU RATHER...LIVE ONE DAY AS A LEECH OR AS A SNAIL?

Player 1   Question Points _____   Laugh Points _____
Player 2   Question Points _____   Laugh Points _____

ROUND 5: EWWWW!

PLAYER 1

_____
Round Total

PLAYER 2

_____
Round Total

_____

ROUND CHAMPION

ROUND 6: PREPARE TO THROW UP

1. WOULD YOU RATHER...MAKE IT A LAW TO FART INTO A JAR OR SNEEZE INTO THE FACE OF THE CLOSEST PERSON?

Player 1   Question Points _____ Laugh Points _____
Player 2   Question Points _____ Laugh Points _____

2. WOULD YOU RATHER... HAVE A TONGUE LIKE A COW OR 100 TEETH?

Player 1   Question Points _____ Laugh Points _____
Player 2   Question Points _____ Laugh Points _____

3. WOULD YOU RATHER...BE SO HUNGRY THAT YOU EAT PLASTIC OR EAT THE SAME MEAL FOR A YEAR?

Player 1   Question Points _____ Laugh Points _____
Player 2   Question Points _____ Laugh Points _____

4. WOULD YOU RATHER...YOUR BLOOD WAS GARLIC BUTTER, OR YOUR SALIVA WAS HONEY?

Player 1   Question Points _____ Laugh Points _____
Player 2   Question Points _____ Laugh Points _____

5. WOULD YOU RATHER...LICK YOURSELF CLEAN OR CLEAN YOURSELF WITH A RAG ON A STICK?

Player 1   Question Points _____ Laugh Points _____
Player 2   Question Points _____ Laugh Points _____

6. WOULD YOU RATHER...HAVE A MASSIVE ITCHY SPOT ON YOUR BUTT OR TOENAILS SO LONG YOU CAN'T WEAR SHOES?

Player 1   Question Points _____ Laugh Points _____
Player 2   Question Points _____ Laugh Points _____

7. WOULD YOU RATHER...SWEAT LOADS WHEN YOU SMILE OR VOMIT WHEN YOU LAUGH?

Player 1   Question Points _____ Laugh Points _____
Player 2   Question Points _____ Laugh Points _____

8. WOULD YOU RATHER...SWAP CLOTHES WITH YOUR PARENTS FOR A DAY OR WEAR THE SAME CLOTHES FOR A WEEK?

Player 1   Question Points _____ Laugh Points _____
Player 2   Question Points _____ Laugh Points _____

9. WOULD YOU RATHER...BE A PET ANACONDA OR A PET TORTOISE?

Player 1   Question Points _____   Laugh Points _____
Player 2   Question Points _____   Laugh Points _____

10. WOULD YOU RATHER... DRINK MUSTARD FOR $50 OR EAT THE WORLD'S HOTTEST CHILI FOR $10,000?

Player 1   Question Points _____   Laugh Points _____
Player 2   Question Points _____   Laugh Points _____

11. WOULD YOU RATHER...CONSUME WARM SUSHI FOR BREAKFAST OR COLD FRIED CHICKEN FOR DINNER?

Player 1   Question Points _____   Laugh Points _____
Player 2   Question Points _____   Laugh Points _____

12. WOULD YOU RATHER...SPEND AN HOUR IN A ROOM FULL OF BANANA PEELS OR 30 MINUTES IN A PORTALOO?

Player 1   Question Points _____   Laugh Points _____
Player 2   Question Points _____   Laugh Points _____

13. WOULD YOU RATHER...WALK A 1KM PATH MADE OF JAM DOUGHNUTS OR JUMP ON A GIANT WHOOPEE CUSHION FULL OF DOG POOP?

Player 1   Question Points _____ Laugh Points _____
Player 2   Question Points _____ Laugh Points _____

14. WOULD YOU RATHER...DECORATE YOUR BEDROOM WALLS IN PEANUT BUTTER OR IN CHOCOLATE SYRUP?

Player 1   Question Points _____ Laugh Points _____
Player 2   Question Points _____ Laugh Points _____

15. WOULD YOU RATHER...EAT 5 DEEP-FRIED TARANTULAS OR ONE BOILED SNAKE?

Player 1   Question Points _____ Laugh Points _____
Player 2   Question Points _____ Laugh Points _____

16. WOULD YOU RATHER...POOP IN A BUSH OR AT A FRIEND'S HOUSE BUT YOU CLOG THE TOILET?

Player 1   Question Points _____ Laugh Points _____
Player 2   Question Points _____ Laugh Points _____

17. WOULD YOU RATHER...LICK A BRICK WALL OR KISS THE GROUND?

Player 1   Question Points _____ Laugh Points _____
Player 2   Question Points _____ Laugh Points _____

18. WOULD YOU RATHER...GO TO WORK IN A COCKROACH-INFESTED OFFICE OR SIT ON A BUS FULL OF MOSQUITOES?

Player 1   Question Points _____ Laugh Points _____
Player 2   Question Points _____ Laugh Points _____

19. WOULD YOU RATHER... PLAY HIDE AND SEEK AT A RUBBISH DUMP OR TAG IN A SEWAGE PLANT?

Player 1   Question Points _____ Laugh Points _____
Player 2   Question Points _____ Laugh Points _____

20. WOULD YOU RATHER...EAT JUNK FOOD FOR A MONTH OR HEALTHY FOOD FOR A WHOLE YEAR?

Player 1   Question Points _____ Laugh Points _____
Player 2   Question Points _____ Laugh Points _____

PLAYER 1

_____
Round Total

PLAYER 2

_____
Round Total

_____
ROUND CHAMPION

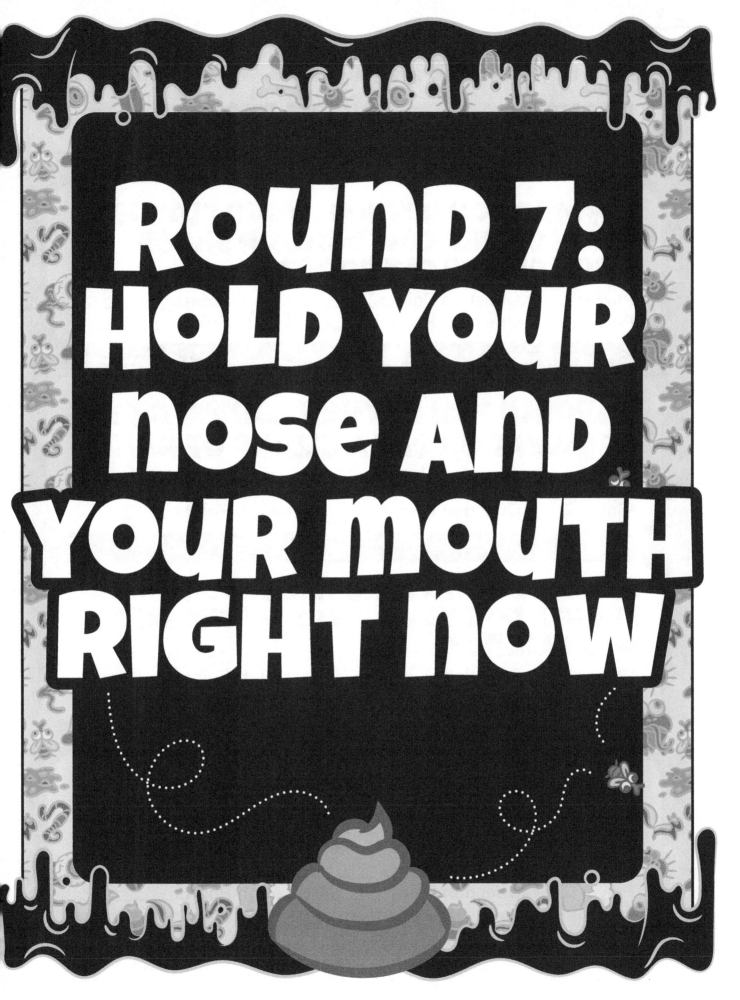

ROUND 7: HOLD YOUR nose AND YOUR MOUTH RIGHT now

1. WOULD YOU RATHER...YOUR CLOTHES SMELLED LIKE COW DUNG OR SHOES SMELLED LIKE CAT POOP?

Player 1   Question Points _____ Laugh Points _____
Player 2   Question Points _____ Laugh Points _____

2. WOULD YOU RATHER...DRINK A PINT OF SWEAT OR EAT A CLUMP OF HAIR?

Player 1   Question Points _____ Laugh Points _____
Player 2   Question Points _____ Laugh Points _____

3. WOULD YOU RATHER...EAT DOG FOOD FROM A DOG BOWL OR SNIFF THE BUTT OF A CANINE?

Player 1   Question Points _____ Laugh Points _____
Player 2   Question Points _____ Laugh Points _____

4. WOULD YOU RATHER...YOUR TEETH WERE MADE OF MARSHMALLOW OR YOUR HAIR WAS MADE OF NOODLES?

Player 1   Question Points _____ Laugh Points _____
Player 2   Question Points _____ Laugh Points _____

5. WOULD YOU RATHER...HAVE TO SMELL A DIRTY DIAPER OR WEAR A DIRTY DIAPER FOR 8 HOURS?

Player 1   Question Points _____ Laugh Points _____
Player 2   Question Points _____ Laugh Points _____

6. WOULD YOU RATHER...HAVE 1 MILLION FRIENDLY ANTS RUN OVER YOUR BODY OR GET STUNG BY 3 WASPS?

Player 1   Question Points _____ Laugh Points _____
Player 2   Question Points _____ Laugh Points _____

7. WOULD YOU RATHER...LET A CATERPILLAR USE YOUR ARM TO MAKE A COCOON OR A MOSQUITO LAY EGGS IN YOUR HAIR?

Player 1   Question Points _____ Laugh Points _____
Player 2   Question Points _____ Laugh Points _____

8. WOULD YOU RATHER...LET ALL YOUR FRIENDS SLEEP IN YOUR BED, AND YOU SLEEP ON THE COUCH, OR YOU SLEEP ON THE COUCH AT A FRIEND'S PLACE?

Player 1   Question Points _____ Laugh Points _____
Player 2   Question Points _____ Laugh Points _____

9. WOULD YOU RATHER...DRINK EXPIRED YOGURT FOR 3 DAYS OR EAT FLIES FOR A WEEK?

Player 1   Question Points _____ Laugh Points _____
Player 2   Question Points _____ Laugh Points _____

10. WOULD YOU RATHER...HAVE A YEAR WITH NO HAIR OR A MONTH WITH NO SENSE OF SMELL?

Player 1   Question Points _____ Laugh Points _____
Player 2   Question Points _____ Laugh Points _____

11. WOULD YOU RATHER...LET A DOG PEE ON YOU OR 5 CATS LICK YOU?

Player 1   Question Points _____ Laugh Points _____
Player 2   Question Points _____ Laugh Points _____

12. WOULD YOU RATHER...SWIM IN A RIVER OF RED WINE OR CLIMB A MOUNTAIN OF RUBBISH?

Player 1   Question Points _____ Laugh Points _____
Player 2   Question Points _____ Laugh Points _____

13. WOULD YOU RATHER...WHEN YOU SHOUT YOU PUKE OR WHEN YOU WHISPER YOU FART LOADS?

Player 1   Question Points _____ Laugh Points _____
Player 2   Question Points _____ Laugh Points _____

14. WOULD YOU RATHER...GET SWARMED BY 10 PIGEONS OR SWARMED BY 3 RATS WHEN YOU GO OUTSIDE?

Player 1   Question Points _____ Laugh Points _____
Player 2   Question Points _____ Laugh Points _____

15. WOULD YOU RATHER...RANDOM PEOPLE JUST TOUCH YOUR FACE OR TOUCH ONE FRIEND WITH HANDS COVERED IN CAT POOP?

Player 1   Question Points _____ Laugh Points _____
Player 2   Question Points _____ Laugh Points _____

16. WOULD YOU RATHER...STUCK IN AN ELEVATOR FULL OF ROTTEN FISH OR ROTTEN EGGS?

Player 1   Question Points _____ Laugh Points _____
Player 2   Question Points _____ Laugh Points _____

51

17. WOULD YOU RATHER...DOGS PEE ON YOU EVERY TIME YOU GO TO THE PARK OR CATS SNEAK INTO YOUR ROOM TO POOP?

Player 1   Question Points _____ Laugh Points _____
Player 2   Question Points _____ Laugh Points _____

18. WOULD YOU RATHER...KISS A ZOMBIE OR HUG A WET WEREWOLF?

Player 1   Question Points _____ Laugh Points _____
Player 2   Question Points _____ Laugh Points _____

19. WOULD YOU RATHER...BE COMPLETELY COVERED IN FEATHERS OR IN HAIR?

Player 1   Question Points _____ Laugh Points _____
Player 2   Question Points _____ Laugh Points _____

20. WOULD YOU RATHER...NIBBLE ON NOSE HAIR OR ON EAR WAX?

Player 1   Question Points _____ Laugh Points _____
Player 2   Question Points _____ Laugh Points _____

PLAYER 1

Round Total

PLAYER 2

Round Total

ROUND CHAMPION

ROUND 8:
SO GROSS!

1. WOULD YOU RATHER...DRINK A PINT OF SOAPY WATER OR A SHOT OF TOILET WATER?

Player 1   Question Points _____   Laugh Points _____
Player 2   Question Points _____   Laugh Points _____

2. WOULD YOU RATHER...SWEAT LOADS DOWN YOUR BACK OR FROM YOUR ARMPITS?

Player 1   Question Points _____   Laugh Points _____
Player 2   Question Points _____   Laugh Points _____

3. WOULD YOU RATHER...EAT A SCAB OR LICK A SPOT ON SOMEONE'S FACE?

Player 1   Question Points _____   Laugh Points _____
Player 2   Question Points _____   Laugh Points _____

4. WOULD YOU RATHER...YOUR MOTHER SNEEZED ON YOUR CLOTHES, OR YOUR DAD PUKED ON YOUR PHONE?

Player 1   Question Points _____   Laugh Points _____
Player 2   Question Points _____   Laugh Points _____

5. WOULD YOU RATHER...A DOG DROOLED ALL OVER YOUR FACE, OR YOU DROOLED OVER A DOG?

Player 1   Question Points _____ Laugh Points _____
Player 2   Question Points _____ Laugh Points _____

6. WOULD YOU RATHER...COUGH HAIRBALLS OR HAVE A LONG DIRTY TAIL?

Player 1   Question Points _____ Laugh Points _____
Player 2   Question Points _____ Laugh Points _____

7. WOULD YOU RATHER...TAKE A SNIFF OF SOMEONE'S ARMPITS FOR $10 OR SUCK ON SOMEONE'S TOE FOR $50?

Player 1   Question Points _____ Laugh Points _____
Player 2   Question Points _____ Laugh Points _____

8. WOULD YOU RATHER...WIPE YOUR BUTT IN PUBLIC OR WIPE SOMEONE ELSE'S BUTT IN PRIVATE?

Player 1   Question Points _____ Laugh Points _____
Player 2   Question Points _____ Laugh Points _____

PLAYER 1 _____   PLAYER 2 _____

9. WOULD YOU RATHER...CATCH A DEAD BUG IN YOUR MOUTH OR PUT A WORM UP YOUR NOSE?

Player 1   Question Points _____ Laugh Points _____
Player 2   Question Points _____ Laugh Points _____

10. WOULD YOU RATHER...WRAP BACON ALL OVER YOUR LEGS OR HAVE PORK CHOPS IN YOUR SHOES?

Player 1   Question Points _____ Laugh Points _____
Player 2   Question Points _____ Laugh Points _____

11. WOULD YOU RATHER...EAT A HANDFUL OF SNOT OR SNIFF CHILI PEPPER SEEDS?

Player 1   Question Points _____ Laugh Points _____
Player 2   Question Points _____ Laugh Points _____

12. WOULD YOU RATHER...HAVE LICE BETWEEN YOUR TEETH OR HAVE YOUR EARS FILLED WITH WORMS?

Player 1   Question Points _____ Laugh Points _____
Player 2   Question Points _____ Laugh Points _____

13. WOULD YOU RATHER...BITE OFF SOMEONE'S NOSE OR BITE OFF AN EAR?

Player 1   Question Points _____ Laugh Points _____
Player 2   Question Points _____ Laugh Points _____

14. WOULD YOU RATHER...GO TO THE TOILET IN A SINK OR IN THE SHOWER?

Player 1   Question Points _____ Laugh Points _____
Player 2   Question Points _____ Laugh Points _____

15. WOULD YOU RATHER...DROP YOUR PHONE IN A BLOCKED TOILET OR LOSE YOUR WALLET IN A BOX FULL OF WASPS?

Player 1   Question Points _____ Laugh Points _____
Player 2   Question Points _____ Laugh Points _____

16. WOULD YOU RATHER...LET BATS SLEEP ABOVE YOUR BED OR SPIDERS SLEEP IN YOUR CLOSET?

Player 1   Question Points _____ Laugh Points _____
Player 2   Question Points _____ Laugh Points _____

17. WOULD YOU RATHER...CHEW ON GUM FOR 3 HOURS OR LICK A BAR OF SOAP FOR 10 MINUTES?

Player 1   Question Points _____ Laugh Points _____
Player 2   Question Points _____ Laugh Points _____

18. WOULD YOU RATHER...EVERY ROOM IN YOUR HOUSE WAS COVERED IN DUST OR SAND?

Player 1   Question Points _____ Laugh Points _____
Player 2   Question Points _____ Laugh Points _____

19. WOULD YOU RATHER...MAKE SCENTED CANDLES FROM YOUR EAR WAX OR MAKE ICE LOLLIES FROM YOUR SPIT?

Player 1   Question Points _____ Laugh Points _____
Player 2   Question Points _____ Laugh Points _____

20. WOULD YOU RATHER...EAT TISSUE PAPER OR ROLL AROUND IN THE MUD?

Player 1   Question Points _____ Laugh Points _____
Player 2   Question Points _____ Laugh Points _____

PLAYER 1

_____
Round Total

PLAYER 2

_____
Round Total

_____

ROUND CHAMPION

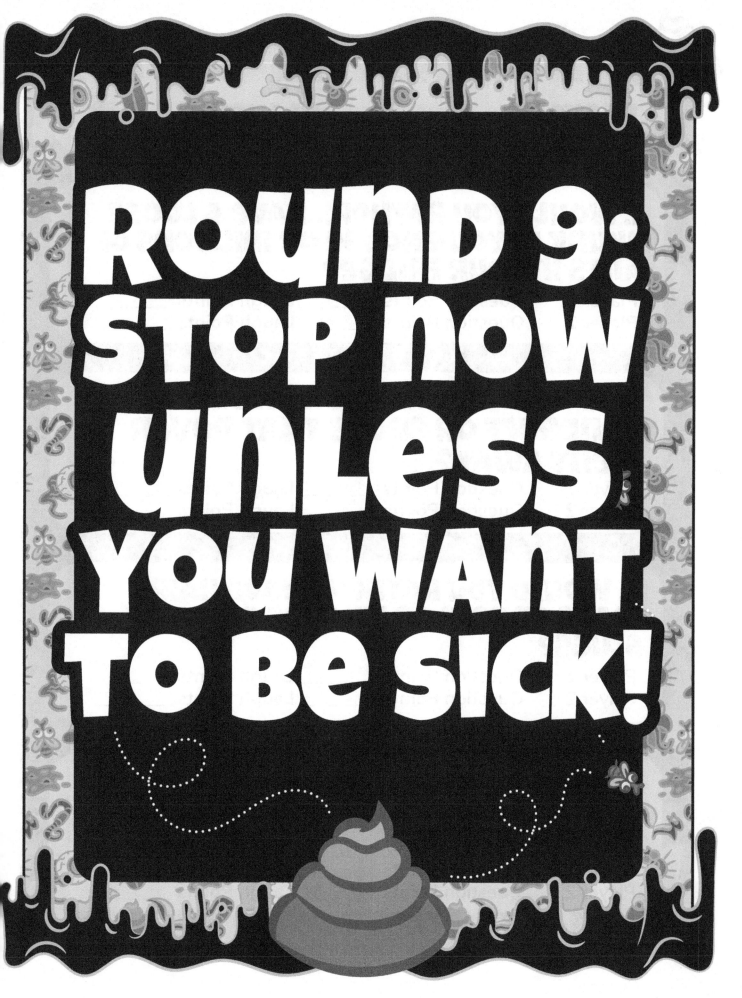

ROUND 9: STOP now UNLESS YOU WANT TO BE SICK!

1. WOULD YOU RATHER...HAVE A LOOSE SKUNK IN YOUR HOUSE OR MILLIONS OF ANTS IN YOUR FRIDGE?

Player 1   Question Points _____ Laugh Points _____
Player 2   Question Points _____ Laugh Points _____

2. WOULD YOU RATHER...HAVE DANDRUFF OR SPOTS THAT NEVER WENT AWAY?

Player 1   Question Points _____ Laugh Points _____
Player 2   Question Points _____ Laugh Points _____

3. WOULD YOU RATHER...HAVE HAIR MADE OF EELS OR FINGERS MADE OF SLUGS?

Player 1   Question Points _____ Laugh Points _____
Player 2   Question Points _____ Laugh Points _____

4. WOULD YOU RATHER...EVERYONE SPITS OR EVERYONE FARTS AT THE DINNER TABLE?

Player 1   Question Points _____ Laugh Points _____
Player 2   Question Points _____ Laugh Points _____

5. WOULD YOU RATHER...LET A MONKEY THROW POOP AT YOU OR A PACK OF WOLVES DROOL ALL OVER YOU?

Player 1   Question Points _____ Laugh Points _____
Player 2   Question Points _____ Laugh Points _____

6. WOULD YOU RATHER...SWIM IN A SWAMP FULL OF HIPPOS OR SIT IN A PADDLING POOL OF JELLYFISH?

Player 1   Question Points _____ Laugh Points _____
Player 2   Question Points _____ Laugh Points _____

7. WOULD YOU RATHER...GO INSIDE THE MOUTH OF A BLUE WHALE OR SLEEP INSIDE A CHICKEN COOP?

Player 1   Question Points _____ Laugh Points _____
Player 2   Question Points _____ Laugh Points _____

8. WOULD YOU RATHER...PREPARE RAW MEAT FOR TIGERS OR MAKE DOG FOOD FROM SCRATCH?

Player 1   Question Points _____ Laugh Points _____
Player 2   Question Points _____ Laugh Points _____

9. WOULD YOU RATHER...HAVE RACCOONS PLAY WITH YOUR GARBAGE EVERY NIGHT OR MICE STOLE FOOD FROM YOUR KITCHEN EVERY MORNING?

Player 1   Question Points _____ Laugh Points _____
Player 2   Question Points _____ Laugh Points _____

10. WOULD YOU RATHER...GET A MASSAGE FROM A WALRUS OR FROM AN OCTOPUS?

Player 1   Question Points _____ Laugh Points _____
Player 2   Question Points _____ Laugh Points _____

11. WOULD YOU RATHER... HAVE 5 WET KOALA BEARS STUCK TO YOUR BODY FOR AN HOUR OR 10 MICE IN YOUR POCKETS FOR 30 MINUTES?

Player 1   Question Points _____ Laugh Points _____
Player 2   Question Points _____ Laugh Points _____

12. WOULD YOU RATHER...BE WRAPPED INSIDE A SNAKESKIN OR COVERED IN FEATHERS WITH GLUE?

Player 1   Question Points _____ Laugh Points _____
Player 2   Question Points _____ Laugh Points _____

13. WOULD YOU RATHER...HAVE GUM ALWAYS STUCK TO YOUR TEETH OR WAKE UP WITH FLEAS EVERY MORNING?

Player 1   Question Points _____ Laugh Points _____
Player 2   Question Points _____ Laugh Points _____

14. WOULD YOU RATHER...FART HONEY OR SNEEZE FROG SPAWN?

Player 1   Question Points _____ Laugh Points _____
Player 2   Question Points _____ Laugh Points _____

15. WOULD YOU RATHER... KISS A TOAD TO TURN INVISIBLE OR LICK A SLUG TO BE ABLE TO FLY?

Player 1   Question Points _____ Laugh Points _____
Player 2   Question Points _____ Laugh Points _____

16. WOULD YOU RATHER...TURN YOUR FAMILY INTO DUNG BEETLES OR YOUR FRIENDS INTO WASPS?

Player 1   Question Points _____ Laugh Points _____
Player 2   Question Points _____ Laugh Points _____

17. WOULD YOU RATHER...YOUR BEDROOM WAS NEXT TO A MEAT FACTORY OR A SEWAGE PLANT?

Player 1   Question Points _____ Laugh Points _____
Player 2   Question Points _____ Laugh Points _____

18. WOULD YOU RATHER...EVERY WINDOW IN YOUR HOUSE HAD SPIDER WEBS OR EVERY ROOM HAD MOTHS?

Player 1   Question Points _____ Laugh Points _____
Player 2   Question Points _____ Laugh Points _____

19. WOULD YOU RATHER...EAT RAT-FLAVORED ICE CREAM OR A PIZZA SLICE WITH SNOT ON IT?

Player 1   Question Points _____ Laugh Points _____
Player 2   Question Points _____ Laugh Points _____

20. WOULD YOU RATHER...HAVE JELLYFISH RAIN FROM THE SKY OR SNAKES ERUPT FROM THE GROUND?

Player 1   Question Points _____ Laugh Points _____
Player 2   Question Points _____ Laugh Points _____

PLAYER 1

Round Total

PLAYER 2

Round Total

ROUND CHAMPION

ROUND 10: THE YUCKIEST, GROSSEST QUESTIONS YOU WILL EVER READ

1. WOULD YOU RATHER...HAND WASH YOUR CLOTHES IN CUSTARD OR IN MAYONNAISE?

Player 1   Question Points _____ Laugh Points _____
Player 2   Question Points _____ Laugh Points _____

2. WOULD YOU RATHER...FIND CIGARETTE BUTTS IN YOUR SOCKS OR WARM COLESLAW IN YOUR SHOES?

Player 1   Question Points _____ Laugh Points _____
Player 2   Question Points _____ Laugh Points _____

3. WOULD YOU RATHER...HAVE NO BATHROOM AND USE A HOLE IN THE GROUND OUTSIDE OR NO BEDROOM AND SLEEP IN A TENT?

Player 1   Question Points _____ Laugh Points _____
Player 2   Question Points _____ Laugh Points _____

4. WOULD YOU RATHER...SOMEONE ALWAYS FARTS REALLY BADLY IN YOUR FACE WHEN YOU ARE ABOUT TO EAT YOUR FAVORITE FOOD OR YOU ALWAYS VOMIT WHEN YOU SMELL YOUR FAVORITE FOOD?

Player 1   Question Points _____ Laugh Points _____
Player 2   Question Points _____ Laugh Points _____

5. WOULD YOU RATHER...DRINK SOUP THAT YOU HAD JUST SWAM IN OR EAT COLD PORRIDGE OFF THE TABLE?

Player 1   Question Points _____   Laugh Points _____
Player 2   Question Points _____   Laugh Points _____

6. WOULD YOU RATHER...GET CAUGHT IN A ROTTEN EGG TORNADO OR IN AN EARTHQUAKE AT A RUBBISH DUMP?

Player 1   Question Points _____   Laugh Points _____
Player 2   Question Points _____   Laugh Points _____

7. WOULD YOU RATHER...MAKE A STATUE FROM UNCOOKED MEAT OR FROM BABY DIAPERS?

Player 1   Question Points _____   Laugh Points _____
Player 2   Question Points _____   Laugh Points _____

8. WOULD YOU RATHER...EAT A DOUGHNUT WITH A BOILED EGG FILLING OR DRINK COKE MIXED WITH MUSTARD?

Player 1   Question Points _____   Laugh Points _____
Player 2   Question Points _____   Laugh Points _____

9. WOULD YOU RATHER...BE ABLE TO DETACH YOUR LIMBS OR PUKE EXPIRED YOGURT?

Player 1   Question Points _____ Laugh Points _____
Player 2   Question Points _____ Laugh Points _____

10. WOULD YOU RATHER...BE ABLE TO SWIM SUPER FAST BY FARTING OR RUN SUPER FAST BY BURPING?

Player 1   Question Points _____ Laugh Points _____
Player 2   Question Points _____ Laugh Points _____

11. WOULD YOU RATHER...SIT ON A PIECE OF GUM ON PUBLIC TRANSPORT OR YOUR HANDS GET DIRTY FROM TOUCHING A KNOB?

Player 1   Question Points _____ Laugh Points _____
Player 2   Question Points _____ Laugh Points _____

12. WOULD YOU RATHER...SWEAT LOADS WHEN YOU SLEEP OR FART LOADS WHEN YOU ARE AWAKE?

Player 1   Question Points _____ Laugh Points _____
Player 2   Question Points _____ Laugh Points _____

13. WOULD YOU RATHER...EAT EVERY PAGE FROM AN OLD LIBRARY BOOK FOR $1000 OR DRINK ANY JUICE FROM THE BOTTOM OF A RUBBISH BIN FOR $10000?

Player 1   Question Points _____ Laugh Points _____
Player 2   Question Points _____ Laugh Points _____

14. WOULD YOU RATHER...HAVE 100 PIGEONS POOP ON YOU OR 50 SPIDERS CLIMB ON YOU?

Player 1   Question Points _____ Laugh Points _____
Player 2   Question Points _____ Laugh Points _____

15. WOULD YOU RATHER...REPLACE SAYING HELLO WITH SPITTING OR REPLACE SAYING GOODBYE WITH A STINKY FART?

Player 1   Question Points _____ Laugh Points _____
Player 2   Question Points _____ Laugh Points _____

16. WOULD YOU RATHER...EAT A STEAK THAT WAS RUBBED UNDER SOMEONE'S ARMPIT OR EAT PIZZA THAT HAS HAIR AS A TOPPING?

Player 1   Question Points _____ Laugh Points _____
Player 2   Question Points _____ Laugh Points _____

17. WOULD YOU RATHER...DRINK VINEGAR OR DRINK CABBAGE JUICE WITH EVERY MEAL?

Player 1   Question Points _____ Laugh Points _____
Player 2   Question Points _____ Laugh Points _____

18. WOULD YOU RATHER...HAVE REALLY BLACK TEETH OR A NOSE WITH 6 NOSTRILS?

Player 1   Question Points _____ Laugh Points _____
Player 2   Question Points _____ Laugh Points _____

19. WOULD YOU RATHER...SHED YOUR SKIN LIKE A SNAKE EVERY MORNING OR YOU GREW LOADS OF HAIR ON YOUR BACK?

Player 1   Question Points _____ Laugh Points _____
Player 2   Question Points _____ Laugh Points _____

20. WOULD YOU RATHER...SUCK ON A RAW MUSHROOM OR SWALLOW A HANDFUL OF SALT?

Player 1   Question Points _____ Laugh Points _____
Player 2   Question Points _____ Laugh Points _____

ROUND 10: THE YUCKIEST, GROSSEST QUESTIONS YOU WILL EVER READ

PLAYER 1

Round Total

PLAYER 2

Round Total

ROUND CHAMPION

1. Ancient Egyptians would remove organs from a body before turning them into a mummy, but how did they retrieve the brain without cutting the skin?

Player 1   Question Points _____ Laugh Points _____
Player 2   Question Points _____ Laugh Points _____

2. The Regal horned lizard, can defend itself by squirting blood out of its body, but where in its tiny scaly body does it squirt blood?

Player 1   Question Points _____ Laugh Points _____
Player 2   Question Points _____ Laugh Points _____

3. Your body can produce enough of what to fill 500 bath tubs in your lifetime?

Player 1   Question Points _____ Laugh Points _____
Player 2   Question Points _____ Laugh Points _____

4. In Ancient Rome, the Romans loved to feast on a special kind of fish known as "licker fish" but what is the Licker fish's super gross main source of food?

Player 1   Question Points _____ Laugh Points _____
Player 2   Question Points _____ Laugh Points _____

5. During the first exploration of America, times were tough. So tough that settlers would do what with squirrels?

Player 1   Question Points _____ Laugh Points _____
Player 2   Question Points _____ Laugh Points _____

6. Flies love to eat everything and anything, but what actually happens when they land on your food?

Player 1   Question Points _____ Laugh Points _____
Player 2   Question Points _____ Laugh Points _____

7. Vultures spend all day in hot weather, but how do they cool themselves off in a hot climate?

Player 1   Question Points _____ Laugh Points _____
Player 2   Question Points _____ Laugh Points _____

8. Hippos are big animals that like to mark their territory, but how do they achieve this?

Player 1   Question Points _____ Laugh Points _____
Player 2   Question Points _____ Laugh Points _____

9. Before the wonderful invention of toothpaste, Ancient Romans would brush their teeth with what incredibly disgusting substance?

Player 1   Question Points _____ Laugh Points _____
Player 2   Question Points _____ Laugh Points _____

10. In ancient Greece and Rome, doctors would help wounded patients by doing what with spiders?

Player 1   Question Points _____ Laugh Points _____
Player 2   Question Points _____ Laugh Points _____

11. Some perfumes and colognes have a splash of ambergris, a substance that is made how?

Player 1   Question Points _____ Laugh Points _____
Player 2   Question Points _____ Laugh Points _____

12. We wake up with stinky breath because the microbes that live in our mouths are busy doing what?

Player 1   Question Points _____ Laugh Points _____
Player 2   Question Points _____ Laugh Points _____

13. If you have gross crusty eyes in the morning, it's because your body was doing what while you slept?

Player 1   Question Points _____ Laugh Points _____
Player 2   Question Points _____ Laugh Points _____

14. The average person farts 14 times a day but do you know how fast those wonderful farts enter the atmosphere?

Player 1   Question Points _____ Laugh Points _____
Player 2   Question Points _____ Laugh Points _____

15. A microbiologist discovered an everyday item that carries 10 times as much bacteria than a toilet seat. Can you guess what it is?

Player 1   Question Points _____ Laugh Points _____
Player 2   Question Points _____ Laugh Points _____

16. In the middle ages, it was completely normal to stop bathing due to warnings from the church as it was seen as immoral. What did Queen Isabella of Castile do about such a crazy idea?

Player 1   Question Points _____ Laugh Points _____
Player 2   Question Points _____ Laugh Points _____

17. What happens when you flush the toilet with the toilet lid up?

Player 1   Question Points _____ Laugh Points _____
Player 2   Question Points _____ Laugh Points _____

18. Lobsters have the incredible ability to go to the toilet in an unusual way, but how?

Player 1   Question Points _____ Laugh Points _____
Player 2   Question Points _____ Laugh Points _____

19. Imagine you are a frog and you ate something really bad. What would you do to feel better?

Player 1   Question Points _____ Laugh Points _____
Player 2   Question Points _____ Laugh Points _____

20. A very hungry tarantula injects its prey with special poison. What happens next?

Player 1   Question Points _____ Laugh Points _____
Player 2   Question Points _____ Laugh Points _____

21. Rabbits love to eat but they do it too quickly! In order for them to get all of the nutrients from a food absorbed, they will do what?

Player 1   Question Points _____ Laugh Points _____
Player 2   Question Points _____ Laugh Points _____

22. Beavers produce a special kind of brown sludge from their castor gland, which is close to their butts. However, what is this sludge often used for?

Player 1   Question Points _____ Laugh Points _____
Player 2   Question Points _____ Laugh Points _____

23. Gelatin is a common product used in gummy candies and wobbly puddings, but where does it actually come from?

Player 1   Question Points _____ Laugh Points _____
Player 2   Question Points _____ Laugh Points _____

24. What popular food can sometimes contain hair, skin, nails and different meats, all combined together?

Player 1   Question Points _____ Laugh Points _____
Player 2   Question Points _____ Laugh Points _____

25. The national dish of Scotland is a special pudding called Haggis, but do you know what's actually in it?

Player 1   Question Points _____ Laugh Points _____
Player 2   Question Points _____ Laugh Points _____

26. Kopi Luwak is one of the most expensive coffees in the world, but do you know the disgusting process involved in making it?

Player 1   Question Points _____ Laugh Points _____
Player 2   Question Points _____ Laugh Points _____

27. Carmine is a special bright red dye used to make red candy, but it's made from crushing up what?

Player 1   Question Points _____ Laugh Points _____
Player 2   Question Points _____ Laugh Points _____

28. Bee vomit is better known as what?

Player 1   Question Points _____ Laugh Points _____
Player 2   Question Points _____ Laugh Points _____

29. Chewing gum originated in Europe around 900 years ago, but it was not strawberry or watermelon or banana flavored. What they chewed on instead was something much worse and tasted like wood, but what was it?

Player 1   Question Points _____ Laugh Points _____
Player 2   Question Points _____ Laugh Points _____

30. In Medieval times, clean water was scarce for battle wounds, but there was a rather gross alternative, urine! But why was urine so special?

Player 1   Question Points _____ Laugh Points _____
Player 2   Question Points _____ Laugh Points _____

31. When people needed dentures back in the 1800s, a time where you had to improvise as technology sucked, dentures were created how?

Player 1   Question Points _____ Laugh Points _____
Player 2   Question Points _____ Laugh Points _____

32. In ancient Rome, people would absorb the power of a fallen Gladiator how?

Player 1   Question Points _____ Laugh Points _____
Player 2   Question Points _____ Laugh Points _____

33. In medieval times, it was believed that illnesses could simply be sucked out in what unusual way?

Player 1   Question Points _____ Laugh Points _____
Player 2   Question Points _____ Laugh Points _____

34. Russian princesses many centuries ago would hire men and women to perform an unusual task with their feet. Can you guess what that is?

Player 1   Question Points _____ Laugh Points _____
Player 2   Question Points _____ Laugh Points _____

35. Mozart was a famous musician, but he also loved writing letters to family members about something really gross, something you wouldn't do in a room full of people. What were the letters about?

Player 1   Question Points _____ Laugh Points _____
Player 2   Question Points _____ Laugh Points _____

36. King Henry II once hired someone called Roland who was a "Flatulist". What did his job involve?

Player 1   Question Points _____ Laugh Points _____
Player 2   Question Points _____ Laugh Points _____

37. The great mystic monk Rasputin was very proud of his unhygienic practices, even once bragging he had not done what for 6 months?

Player 1   Question Points _____ Laugh Points _____
Player 2   Question Points _____ Laugh Points _____

38. In ancient Egypt, having a mashed-up pig's eye poured into your ear was believed to do what?

Player 1   Question Points _____ Laugh Points _____
Player 2   Question Points _____ Laugh Points _____

39. During the Black Plague, doctors would treat boils by?

Player 1   Question Points _____ Laugh Points _____
Player 2   Question Points _____ Laugh Points _____

40. King Henry VIII employed servants for a position of incredible honor, known as the Grooms of the Stool. When the King went to the bathroom, they had to...?

Player 1   Question Points _____ Laugh Points _____
Player 2   Question Points _____ Laugh Points _____

41. In ancient Egypt, there was a practice known as scatomancy, which was the ability to see into the future how?

Player 1   Question Points _____ Laugh Points _____
Player 2   Question Points _____ Laugh Points _____

42. The ancient Romans used what yellow (and sometimes clear) substance to not only whiten their teeth but wash their clothes?

Player 1   Question Points _____ Laugh Points _____
Player 2   Question Points _____ Laugh Points _____

43. The average jar of peanut butter is believed to possibly contain what?

Player 1   Question Points _____ Laugh Points _____
Player 2   Question Points _____ Laugh Points _____

44. The ancient Romans loved condiments like we do today; however, they had one called "Garum" which was made from?

Player 1   Question Points _____ Laugh Points _____
Player 2   Question Points _____ Laugh Points _____

45. In Greenland, the native Inuits make a special wintertime food called Kiviak. To make this, they would get a seal's skin and stuff it with what?

Player 1   Question Points _____ Laugh Points _____
Player 2   Question Points _____ Laugh Points _____

46. The near-blind and toothless hagfish have a disgusting way to eat other dead fish but how?

Player 1   Question Points _____ Laugh Points _____
Player 2   Question Points _____ Laugh Points _____

47. In India, many snapping turtles are released into the Ganges river to help do what?

Player 1   Question Points _____ Laugh Points _____
Player 2   Question Points _____ Laugh Points _____

48. What is a fecal transplant?

Player 1   Question Points _____ Laugh Points _____
Player 2   Question Points _____ Laugh Points _____

49. How do Capuchin monkeys keep their hands and feet clean?

Player 1   Question Points _____ Laugh Points _____
Player 2   Question Points _____ Laugh Points _____

50. The Tasmanian Devil, which lives close to Australia, has a diet made up of small prey but they mostly feast on what?

Player 1   Question Points _____ Laugh Points _____
Player 2   Question Points _____ Laugh Points _____

DOUBLE BONUS TRIVIA ANSWERS

1. A hook was inserted into the nose, and they yanked out the brain
2. From its eyes.
3. Spit
4. Pieces of poop
5. Catch them, cook them and eat them.
6. They vomit saliva to break down the food and then suck it up with their tongues.
7. They poop all over their legs.
8. By throwing big balls of stinky poop at their enemies.
9. A paste made from powdered mouse brains.
10. Using their spider webs as bandages.
11. When a whale vomits in the ocean.
12. Looking for leftover food between our teeth at night, then multiple and release stinky gases.
13. Built a collection of mucus, tears and dead skin.
14. Around 7 miles per hour.
15. Your smartphone.
16. She only took two baths in her entire life.
17. Lots of invisible and gross germs are sent flying out, even as far as five or six feet.
18. They pee out of their faces. Male lobsters fight each other by peeing on each other.
19. Throw up your entire stomach and fling out anything in there before swallowing it again.
20. The prey's insides turn to liquid and the tarantula sucks the yummy insides out.
21. Eat their poop, sometimes even three times.
22. In food as a vanilla substitute.
23. It's from collagen, which is extracted from the skin, bones and connective tissues of animals.

24. Hot dogs.
25. The liver, heart and lung of a sheep wrapped inside it's stomach.
26. An Asian Palm Civet eats the coffee beans and then the beans pooped out are made into coffee.
27. Crushing up insects.
28. Honey
29. Bark from a birch tree.
30. Urine was believed to be a great antiseptic.
31. Dentists made them from the teeth of deceased soldiers.
32. Drinking their fresh, warm blood.
33. By letting a leech suck out the "bad" blood.
34. They were employed as full-time foot ticklers.
35. How great his farts were.
36. Entertaining the king with farts.
37. Change his underpants.
38. Cure blindness.
39. Rubbing them with human poop.
40. Wipe his butt.
41. By looking at someone's poop.
42. Urine.
43. 4 or more rodent hairs.
44. Rotten fish guts.
45. Around 500 small birds which are left to rot over a period of 3 months before it's ready to eat.
46. They slime inside and eat it from inside out.
47. Eat rotting corpses that float in the river.
48. Putting healthy poop into the bottom of a sick person
49. By washing them in their own urine.
50. Already dead animals.

DOUBLE BONUS TRIVIA
PLAYER 1

_____
Round Total

PLAYER 2

_____
Round Total

_____
ROUND CHAMPION

TOTAL SCORES

PLAYER 1

ROUND 1 _____

ROUND 2 _____

ROUND 3 _____

ROUND 4 _____

ROUND 5 _____

ROUND 6 _____

ROUND 7 _____

ROUND 8 _____

ROUND 9 _____

ROUND 10 _____

DOUBLE BONUS
TRIVIA _____

TOTAL _____

PLAYER 2

ROUND 1 _____

ROUND 2 _____

ROUND 3 _____

ROUND 4 _____

ROUND 5 _____

ROUND 6 _____

ROUND 7 _____

ROUND 8 _____

ROUND 9 _____

ROUND 10 _____

DOUBLE BONUS
TRIVIA _____

TOTAL _____

LEADER OF LAUGHTER CERTIFICATE

Made in United States
North Haven, CT
04 April 2023

35025458R00057